Robert Shaw Hutton

A Present Saviour

Great truths for earnest times

Robert Shaw Hutton

A Present Saviour
Great truths for earnest times

ISBN/EAN: 9783337314019

Printed in Europe, USA, Canada, Australia, Japan

Cover: Foto ©Lupo / pixelio.de

More available books at **www.hansebooks.com**

A PRESENT SAVIOUR;

OR,

GREAT TRUTHS FOR EARNEST TIMES.

BY THE REV. R. S. HUTTON, M. A.

PUBLISHED BY THE
AMERICAN TRACT SOCIETY,
150 NASSAU-STREET, NEW YORK.

CONTENTS.

INTRODUCTORY—EARNEST TIMES 5

I.—DANGER 9

II.—ASLEEP 13

III.—A PRISONER OF HOPE 17

IV.—PEACE, PEACE! 21

V.—ONE AT THE DOOR 25

VI.—AWAKENED 29

VII.—WHAT MUST I DO TO BE SAVED? 33

VIII.—JESUS 37

IX.—THE REFUGE 41

X.—A PRESENT SALVATION 45

XI.—COME 49

XII.—NOW 53

XIII.—BUT— 57

XIV.—A FULL SURRENDER 61

XV.—BORN AGAIN 65

4 CONTENTS.

XVI.—A CHRISTIAN -------------------------- 69

XVII.—SECRET THINGS----------------------- 73

XVIII.—THE RACE -------------------------- 77

XIX.—REDEEMING THE TIME --------------- 81

XX.—AN UNCHANGEABLE SAVIOUR--------- 85

XXI.—THE DAY OF SMALL THINGS---------- 89

XXII.—THE FINAL DAY---------------------- 93

A PRESENT SAVIOUR.

INTRODUCTORY.

EARNEST TIMES.

THESE are earnest days in which we live. There is much life in the church. The Spirit is being poured out, and many are being gathered in to Christ. Revivals used to be looked upon as rare things of the past; but now a marvellous work of grace is going on in all parts of the earth, and among races the most distinct. Surely this indicates the dawn of a bright and glorious day.

It is a time of *much prayer*. Never were there so many fervent suppliants at the throne of grace as now. The power of prayer is being recognized. Men are looking on it as a real thing; they are using it as such, and they are drawing down on the church showers of blessings. What answers to prayer are being received! Nor is this a matter to be wondered at. God has been taken at his word; he has been applied to with faith and earnestness, and he has done great things for us, whereof we are glad.

Again, it is a time of *earnest effort*. Much is being done. The grand truth is being widely felt—to every man his work. Young converts have been full of zeal and love. They have set themselves to the duty of doing something for Christ; and how much has been accomplished by them through the length and breadth of the land. Many of these may have received but a slender education; they may have had no great powers of speech; they may have been often spoken against; but they have been ardent in their longings to do good to souls; they have persevered in self-sacrificing labors; and not a few of them have in their respective spheres seen great results. A noble lesson to all believers. Let every one whose heart has been touched with the love of Christ do what he can: let him endeavor to promote humbly and perseveringly the cause of Christ, and he will in no wise lose his reward. Life, says Fuller, is to be measured by action, not by time: a man may die old at thirty, and young at eighty; the one lives after death, the other perished before he died.

It is a time of *great responsibility*. What opportunities for doing good are within the reach of every Christian. The fields are white unto the harvest. How earnest the laborers should be. Never was there such a season of working for Christ. All God's faithful people should be up and doing. And what a time for the unconverted. They are in a Christless state; they hope, however, to be converted before they die; but *when,* if not *now?* Many others are being awakened, while they remain asleep. Many others are yielding to the claims of Jesus, while they are resisting the influences of his grace. Many others are being brought to a saving knowledge of the truth, while they are still living on in indifference to the interests of their souls. If they be not moved at such a time as this, the probability is they will never be moved at all.

How is it with you? If religion be any thing, it is every thing. If it be important at all, it is all-important. If it demand any concern, it demands your supreme concern. Are you judging thus, and acting accordingly? I would have you sit down quietly and consider this matter. Make it the subject of earnest thought, and deal with it as one who knows the vast interests at stake. A Christian traveller tells us that he saw the following admonition printed on a folio sheet in an inn in Savoy, and it was found, he learned, in every house in the district: "Understand well the force of the words—a God, a moment, an eternity: a God who sees you, a moment which flies from you, an eternity which awaits you; a God whom you serve so ill, a moment of which you so little profit, an eternity which you hazard so rashly."

> Grace is flowing like a river;
>   Millions there have been supplied;
> Still it flows as fresh as ever
>   From the Saviour's wounded side.

I.

DANGER.

"It is a fearful thing to fall into the hands of the living God." HEB. 10:31.

IF unconverted, you are in a state of fearful peril. It might well make the blood run cold to think of it. You are every moment exposed to eternal death. Have you no saving interest in the Lord Jesus Christ? Are you not born again? Have you undergone no change of heart? Then I must plainly tell you and fairly warn you of your state. You are under sentence of condemnation. You are subject to the wrath of God. You are liable to the pains of hell.

What keeps the sinner out of that world of misery? Nothing but the mere will of God. He is in the hands of God. At every hour he is dependent for existence on God. Let God speak the word, and he is landed in hell. No one can help him. He is very feebleness. As

easily as you crush a worm, so easily can God
crush a sinner. Is he safe a moment, then?
There are numberless ways in which he may
die. Eternity is very near him. There is but
a step between him and death, and there is but
a step between him and hell. He may be now
in health and strength. He may have his plans
laid down for the future. He may think that
the day of death is still far off. But there are
ever flying around him the unseen shafts of
death. One of these may suddenly strike him
down. And then all is lost. How many are
deploring to-day their unutterable folly. They
had means of grace. They had the gospel
offer. They were told of their danger and of
the way of escape. But they are dead and
gone to hell. And how so? They rejected
Christ. They lived on in worldliness and sin.
They died unsaved. No doubt they had serious thoughts at times. They never intended
to go to the place of misery. They thought
it would be far otherwise with them. But
death came suddenly and unexpectedly, and
they are left to mourn with bitter grief over
their hopeless state. *Life's little day is to deter-*

mine the character of man's eternity. And yet the sinner has not yet begun the mighty work given him to do. Is not this a strange thing indeed? Think of eternal woe. Think of the millions of millions of ages in which the wrath of the Lamb is to be endured. Think of the terrible hopelessness of the damned. All that I can possibly say of it comes infinitely short of the truth. But to all this the sinner is exposed. He may be near the end of his stay on earth. The sun may have shone on him for the last time. Never may he hear another call of mercy. The arrow may be on the wing that is to cut him down. To-morrow he may be in his coffin.

How is it with your soul? Do think on it. Are you safe for eternity? Have you heartily embraced the Saviour and turned to God? Is your salvation sure through living faith in Christ? Have you found peace? How strangely solemn are such questions. They concern your well-being for ever and ever. If you have yet no hope in Christ, it becomes you to bestir yourself at once. Soon may the door of mercy be shut. This very night your soul may be

required of you.   Philip Henry said to some
of his neighbors, who came to see him on
his death-bed, " Oh, make sure work for your
souls, by getting an interest in Christ while
you are in health.   If I had that work to do
now, what would become of me ?   I bless God
I am satisfied.   See to it, all of you, that your
work be not undone when your time is done,
lest you be undone for ever."

Then what my thoughts design to do,
My hands with all your might pursue,
Since no device nor work is found,
Nor faith nor hope beneath the ground.

There are no acts of pardon passed
In the cold grave to which we haste;
But darkness, death, and long despair
Reign in eternal silence there.

II.

ASLEEP.

"What meanest thou, O sleeper? Arise, call upon thy God." JONAH 1:6.

THE sinner asleep! Nay, is he not wide awake? is he not active, busy, full of life? So far as the world is concerned, this is true. He moves about engrossed with earthly cares. And yet in regard to spiritual and eternal things he is in a dead sleep.

Sleep is a state of *darkness;* and the sinner is in such a state. There are scales on his eyes. Satan hath blinded him. He sees not things in their true light. Sin, how odious it is! but he does not see its vileness. Holiness, how attractive it is! but he does not see its beauty. The soul, how inexpressibly valuable it is! but he does not see its worth. Christ, how altogether lovely he is! but he does not see His preciousness. Salvation, how infinitely important it is! but he does not see its unutterable excellency. The pure and piercing eye of God is ever on him. Above him heaven unveils its glories. Hell yawns at his very feet. But all is darkness to him.

Sleep is a state of *insensibility;* and the sinner is in such a state. God speaks to him, calls him, pleads with him. Jesus knocks at his door and seeks admittance. The Holy Ghost draws near and whispers in his ear many a word of warning, invitation, and promise. But no response is given.

Sleep is a state of *dreams;* and the sinner is in such a state. He is taken up with shadows and trifles, and walks in a vain show. He may get a passing glimpse of the grand realities of life, God, Christ, eternity; but he soon falls back into dream-land again. Just look at him. He is poor, penniless, sunk in hopeless bankruptcy; but he fancies he is rich and increased in goods, and in need of nothing. He is away from the light and peace and security of home; but he fancies he is within reach of all that is required to satisfy his heart. A sentence of condemnation has been passed on him; but he fancies he has nothing to fear. He is on the very brink of a dark and unprovided-for eternity; but he fancies that all is well with him.

Sleep is a state of *inactivity:* and the sinner is in such a state. What, is he not full of energy? See with what earnestness he toils for bread, or power, or money. Who shall say that he does nothing? But what is he doing for his soul? Nothing at all. What is he doing for the highest interests of his fellowmen? They may go down to the pit, so far as he is concerned. What is he doing for God— that God who made him; that God in whom he lives and moves and has his being; that God who sent his own dear Son to die for sinners? He bears no love to him, and performs no service for him. What is he doing to prepare for death? It hardly costs him a thought. What is he doing for eternity? He is making the most of time, and leaving eternity to take care of itself.

How is it with you? Are you asleep? If so, awake, I beseech you. You may suppose that you are safe enough; you may see no need of being disturbed; you may fancy that there is no reason why you should be afraid: but

how true the remark of President Edwards:
" While unconverted, you stand over the mouth
of hell by a single plank, and that plank is
rotten." And you *must* awake some day. No
one can sleep on for ever. There is to be a
universal awakening of the body, and there is
to be a universal awakening of the soul. It
will be well for you to awake now. If you
do not, a terrible awakening will come—an
awakening to the awful realities of a lost eternity.

> Since on this wingèd hour
>   Eternity is hung,
> Waken by thine almighty power
>   The aged and the young.

III.

A PRISONER OF HOPE.

"Turn ye to the strong-hold, ye prisoners of hope."
ZECH. 9 : 12.

THE sinner is a prisoner; there are chains that bind him. He is a captive slave. Most pitiable state! But provision has been made for his deliverance. A strong-hold is within his reach. He may turn to it and enjoy the sweets of liberty.

Man was not a prisoner *once*. No chains were about him when he walked in a sinless paradise. He had all the bearing and all the feelings of a free man. True, he was the servant of God. But this in no degree interfered with his liberty. Jehovah's service was felt to be perfect freedom. But how different now! Sin and Satan lord it over him. He may not see and feel his fetters; he may boast of his freedom; he may scorn the idea of being a prisoner and a slave. It was so with the Jews. They were offended with Christ speaking to them about the truth making them free. They answered, "We are Abraham's seed, and were never in bondage to any man: how sayest thou, we shall be made free?" And it is so now. Man in his unawakened state is not conscious of his thraldom, and has no desire to be free. This is the most melancholy thing about the sinner. He is bewitched. He is in a condition of terrible insensibility. You seldom hear from him a murmur against the tyranny of Satan's rule.

But the sinner is *a prisoner of hope.* His condition may be changed; no necessity binds him down to his present state. There are other prisoners in the universe in a far worse condition. For them there is no hope; but they are prisoners of despair. Oh, what a world of misery is hell! It is the region of outer darkness. But surely this must be the most bitter element in the cup of wrath which its inmates are called to drink, that there is for them no hope. The great gulf cannot be crossed by any angel of mercy; the bars of the prison-house cannot be withdrawn; no dawn can break on the long and dreary night. You

cannot tell me the number of the blades of
grass that clothe the mountain-side; you cannot tell me the number of the stars which light
up the arch of heaven; you cannot tell me the
number of the grains of sand which lie on
ocean's shores: but all this you could do far
sooner than tell me the number of the ages of
a lost eternity. *For ever* is written in blazing
characters on the portals of hell. But it is
not so with the sinner now; he may be free.

One has come *preaching deliverance* to the
captive, and the opening of the prison to them
that are bound. The Lord Jesus Christ is
stronger than the strong man who keeps the
sinner in servitude. We have but to turn to
him—to look to him—to betake ourselves to
him, and we are safe. If the Son make us
free, we are free indeed: not that all the
sweets of spiritual liberty are enjoyed on
earth; some traces of his former state of bondage cling to the believer till his dying day;
but he anticipates a glorious future, and even
now he can sing with holy David, "Our soul is
escaped as a bird out of the snare of the fowl-
er: the snare is broken, and we are escaped."

How is it with you? Are you still tied and bound with the chains of sin? Have you not yet turned to the strong-hold? Are you not united by living faith to the Lord Jesus Christ? Is it wise, is it safe to continue a day longer in such a state? This is the time of deliverance. To-morrow the possibility of freedom may be beyond your reach.

He comes the prisoners to release,
  In Satan's bondage held;
The gates of brass before him burst,
  The iron fetters yield.

IV.

PEACE, PEACE!

"They have healed also the hurt of the daughter of my people slightly, saying, Peace, peace; when there is no peace." JER. 6:14.

You may be in a state of carnal security. You may be fancying that all is well; you may be supposing that you have no grounds for fear; you may be indulging the idea that your soul is safe, and yet all the while you may be in a state of condemnation. You may be saying, "Peace, peace," when there is no peace. This may be a true description of your state before God.

Very many are at peace *just because they never seriously think about the salvation of their soul.* Foster says, There is nothing which we shall regret so much, when we have left this world, as our want of thought. How true will this be of such as are careless about their spiritual condition. They are engrossed with other matters; business, pleasures, family cares occupy their minds and hearts, and they never bestow a half-hour's earnest thought on their highest, their eternal interests. How terribly will their peace be broken up!

Very many are at peace, *because they are resting on mistaken notions* of the grounds of a sinner's acceptance with God. They are orthodox in their views, and can talk fluently on the doctrines of the gospel. They bear a character for respectability and godliness. Their hopes for eternity are built on these things. But how ruinous such a notion. A man may have an orthodox head, and yet have the devil in his heart. A man may have his name in the list of the members of the church, and yet not have his name in the Lamb's book of life. A man may pass through the world and make a fair profession, and yet after all be lost. "All that you can tell me," said one on a dying bed, " I have long known well; but I tell you I have lived without real religion. I was forward in the church, but fixed in the world; and my profession only serves to terrify me."

True peace is a most blessed thing. It is a peace which comes from God, and which the world cannot give. It is a peace which may be felt. It is a peace which passes all understanding. And whence does it flow? From a sense of forgiven sin, and acceptance with God through Jesus Christ. Christianity, says Luther, consists in personal pronouns; and never can a human soul have real and abiding peace till it can call Jesus *my* Lord and *my* God, and can feel, Jesus died not only for others, but for *me*.

Have you this peace? Did you ever hear Jesus say in the depths of your troubled heart, "Your sins are forgiven you?" Is he your personal Saviour and friend? Hear and weigh well what godly Rutherford says, "Oh, make your heaven sure, and try how you came by conversion. It is wisdom in you to be plain, honest, sharp with your soul. Remember what peace with God in Christ will be to you when you come to the black and swelling river of death. Let me entreat of you, by your appearance before the dreadful, sin-avenging Judge of the world, to make your accounts ready: read them ere you come to the waterside. It were not amiss to think, What if it come to this—that I have no portion but outer darkness, and be banished from the presence of the Lord, and be given over to the power of the second death? Put yourself by supposition in such a case, and consider what horror will take hold of your poor soul. This is the accepted time; this is the day of salvation. There are many weary heads lying on Christ's bosom, and there is room for yours among the rest." Think well on these solemn words; examine anxiously the grounds of your peace. There is but one foundation for the sinner's hope—the Lord Jesus Christ. See that you have a saving interest in him. I know no other resting-place for a guilty soul. On that foundation alone can it have security and peace.

> Convince us of our sin,
> Then lead to Jesus' blood;
> And to our wondering view reveal
> The secret love of God.

V.

ONE AT THE DOOR.

"Behold, I stand at the door and knock." REV. 3:20.

THE soul is represented in Scripture under the figure of a house; and a noble house it originally was. It was built of polished stones. It was proportioned with exquisite skill. It was a masterpiece of work. And there was one thing which more than any other ennobled it—it was the residence of God. But how different the soul in its natural state now. Sin has marred its glory. God has been excluded from it. With a few lingering traces of its primeval grandeur, it is dark and ruinous and foul. But what a strange sight you have here. God has not utterly destroyed the soul. In his infinite condescension and pitifulness he desires to repair its ruins, and to dwell in it again. And lo, in the person of his Son he is represented as standing at the door of it, and seeking admission. He knows that it is sadly

changed from what it was—that it is full of
darkness and discord and enmity; but he
would have you turn the rusty lock and open
the door, that he may fill all its chambers with
light and music and joy.

The Son of God stands at the sinner's door.
Marvellous spectacle! The Lord of glory
seeking admission into a human heart! And
yet so it is; just because you are a sinner he is
there. He knows your needs; and in love past
finding out, he comes to befriend and bless you.
You are poor, he would enrich you; you are
hungry and thirsty, he would feed you and give
you drink; you are covered with rags, he
would clothe you with a robe of righteousness;
you are blind, he would give you sight; you
are afflicted with a terrible disease, he would
cure you and make you whole. Did ever friend
come to your door laden with such blessings as
these?

The Son of God *stands* at the sinner's door.
He does not wait till you seek him, he comes
to you; he draws near to your very heart.
Has he been long standing there? Let con-
science answer. Many a year perhaps; but

he has not yet gone away. You may have been coldly indifferent to his presence, and may have turned a deaf ear to his gentle voice; but he is waiting still. And now his limbs are weary of standing, and his hands are weary of knocking, and his voice is weary of pleading, and soon may he leave the door.

The Son of God *knocks.* Listen! his hand is on the door. He would awaken you and make you open to him. By *his holy word* he knocks. It gives you many a warning, and presents you with many a promise. By *the dispensations of his providence* he knocks. Are your worldly plans succeeding, and is your home full of gladness? Daily mercies have a voice; they bid you open the door. Are you lying on a bed of sickness? Have you met with some severe loss? Has the grave just closed over some dear object of your love? Trials have a voice. They bid you open the door. By *his Spirit* he knocks. He is doing so with peculiar urgency at the present day; and not in vain. The door of many a soul is opening, and Jesus is entering in.

Are you still treating Jesus with cold neglect? Is your door still shut against him? Does he still stand without? Oh what ingratitude and folly and guilt! His gentle form was bruised for you; his hands and his feet were nailed for you to a cruel cross; his voice cried for you, " My soul is exceeding sorrowful, even unto death." To keep the door shut against him, is not this ingratitude? He would give you all you need. He would free you from evil in every form. He would make you fully and for ever happy. To keep the door shut against him, is not this consummate folly? You are bound to love and honor and serve him. To keep the door shut against him, is not this damning guilt?

> Sovereign of souls, the Prince of peace,
> Oh may thy gentle reign increase;
> Throw wide the door, each willing mind,
> And be his empire all mankind.

VI.

AWAKENED.

"Now when they heard this, they were pricked in their heart." Acts 2:37.

HAVE you been awakened? Have your eyes been opened to your true state as a sinner before God? Do you see and feel your guilt and folly and danger? It is well. You may be troubled. Fear and trembling may fill your heart. It may be a time of deep and sore distress; but surely this is better than to live on asleep: better to awake on earth than to awake in hell.

I do *not wonder at your distress*. What have you been doing? You have been living in the world without God—that God in whom you live and move and have your being. You have been neglecting a loving Saviour, who shed for you his precious blood. You have been resisting the strivings of the Holy Ghost. You have been spending your time wholly taken up with the world that now is, and giving little or no heed to the vast interests of the world to come. You have been forgetting the grand end of your existence upon earth. Do you now see your unspeakable folly? If so, I am not astonished at your being sad in heart. Not to have loved God; not to have received the Saviour; not to have welcomed the Spirit's influences; not to have prized salvation; not to have attended to your precious soul: how great such guilt!

But it is *not enough to be awakened.* Many in your state never obtain salvation. Tears and sorrow cannot take to heaven. I have known not a few once in great distress about their sins who have fallen back into a state of utter indifference. They were pricked in heart; they were deeply moved; you saw in their countenance the signs of great inward trouble; it seemed as if the new birth had taken place in them. We hoped that they were truly converted and brought to Christ: but the world got hold of them again; and now they are as unconcerned about eternal things as ever. You think it can never be so with you. Your feel-

ings are warm; and you fancy that for you to
fall back into a state of indifference is utterly
impossible. Well, then cherish your convictions; seek to have an abiding sense of your
sinfulness; get still blacker views of your unbelief, ingratitude, and selfishness. Beware
lest a thoughtless world should persuade you
that all this uneasiness is uncalled for; but let
it be your most earnest desire to have a deep
sense of your low and lost condition before
God.

And remember that *if you lose your present
convictions*, and be finally lost, it will be far
worse for you than it would otherwise have
been. To think in eternity on days of awakening, on times of sorrow for sin, on occasions
when you gave yourself to prayer and serious
thought, and to think that you afterwards
allowed yourself to fall back into a state of
indifference and worldliness, will not this
immensely aggravate the bitterness of your
future doom? Listen to the solemn words of
McCheyne: " Be not content with half work.
Never rest without converting grace. Make a
full surrender of your soul to God. Halt not

between two opinions. Decide to be altogether Christ's. If you come just up to the gate of heaven, and see the streets of shining gold and the happy faces of the glorious ones who walk there; if you hear their songs, loud as the voice of many waters, sweet as the harpers harping on their harps; and yet, if the gate be shut against you, and Christ say, 'I know you not,' what words can tell the agony with which you will go away to lie down in sorrow—to lie down in hell? If there be one wailing cry from that sad abode more dismal than another, it will be the bitter wailing of the almost Christian."

Is there a thing beneath the sun,
   That strives with thee my heart to share?
Ah, tear it hence, and reign alone,
   The Lord of every motion there.
Then shall my heart from earth be free,
When it hath found repose in thee.

VII. ˗

WHAT MUST I DO TO BE SAVED?

"He came trembling, and fell down before Paul and Silas, and said, Sirs, what must I do to be saved?" Acts 16:29, 30.

WHAT a solemn question! It is the cry of an awakened sinner. And how momentous his inquiry. He has got a view of his guilt and his danger. He knows that before him is a dark eternity, and beneath him an angry hell, and he looks around for deliverance from his perilous position. Whence is relief to come?

Some in the dark regions of heathendom are offering costly sacrifices. They are heaping on a rude pile bleeding victims. They are subjecting themselves to painful acts of self-denial, and giving of the fruit of their body for the sin of their soul. They are trusting to these modes of propitiating the anger of an offended God. Vain notion. The favor of the Almighty is not to be secured thus. Others, again, are making a fair profession. They are regular in their attendance on ordinances. They are professing members of the Christian church. They are respectable religionists. Because of this they expect to be saved. Vain notion. Not thus can they inherit the kingdom of heaven. Others are depending on the unblemished moral character they bear. They are good citizens. They are kind and generous friends. They are well-disposed neighbors. All this will go so far, they think, and Christ's merits will make up the difference. Vain notion. By no such piece of patchwork as this is man to be saved.

A woman called one day on Dr. Chalmers in great distress of mind. "Oh, doctor," said she, "what must I *do* to get peace?" "*Do?*" replied he; "nothing." "Nothing?" replied the disappointed inquirer; "nothing? Is that all the comfort you have for me?" "Yes, that is all; you have nothing to do, but you have something to *take*. It's all done. Christ has done it. He has bought a pardon and peace for you, and you have got to take it." "I see it, I see it," replied the woman joyfully, and left in peace.

Do *you* see it? There is no mystery about it. It is a simple, though great and wondrous redemptive scheme. Jesus the eternal Son of God became your surety. He made a mighty stoop; he left heaven; he clothed himself in robes of clay, and came to earth; he stood in your room and stead; he obeyed the whole law for you; he suffered for you an ignominious death, and bore the penalty your sins deserved; he wrought out for you a perfect righteousness. And now from his throne in glory he says to you, "Believe on me as your Saviour; look upon God as your reconciled Father through me; ask of him to accept of you because of my obedience and death: thus seek to be one with me; regard me as your salvation; cast yourself for eternity on me: do this, and live for ever."

Look away from yourself in the great matter of acceptance with God. You have nothing to do but to trust. Faith in Jesus Christ to save is the way to heaven. A certain anxious inquirer could not get peace. Her convictions of sin were deep and clear. She assented to all the doctrines of grace. She

sought earnestly to attain salvation. But she
could get no comfort for a time. At length
she came to a friend, and told him she had
made a new discovery. On being asked what
it was she had found out, she replied that the
way of salvation all seemed to her now perfectly plain; that the darkness was gone, and
that she saw now what she never saw before.
On the question being put to her what she saw
now, she said, "Don't you think the reason
why we do not get out of darkness sooner, is
that we don't believe? As you were reading a hymn last night, I saw the whole way of
salvation perfectly plain, and wondered that I
had never seen it before. I saw that I had
nothing whatever to do but to trust in Christ.
The verses which brought me to peace were
these:

> My soul obeys the almighty call,
>   And runs to this relief;
> I would believe thy promise, Lord,
>   Oh help mine unbelief.
>
> A guilty, weak, and helpless worm,
>   On thy kind arms I fall;
> Be thou my strength and righteousness,
>   My Jesus and my all.

VIII.

JESUS.

"Thou shalt call his name JESUS; for he shall save his people from their sins." MATT. 1:21.

WHAT a precious name is the name of Jesus. How sweet and soothing and joyous. To how many weary hearts it affords refreshment and rest. It means Saviour, and Jesus saves his people from their sins. They are guilty; but he saves them from guilt. They are unholy; but he saves them from the power of indwelling iniquity. They are by nature liable to the punishment of eternal death; but he saves them from all the woful consequences of the fall.

Jesus can save you from the *guilt of sin.* That guilt exposes you to the wrath and curse of God. It renders you liable to hell. Because of it you are in danger of all the miseries of everlasting death. Whither can you flee for security?

There is but one shelter for the soul—Jesus

Christ. Repair to him; put your trust in him; secure by faith a saving interest in him. In that case all is well; the stains of guilt are washed away in his atoning blood; you are accepted of God; he regards you with complacency; you are his for ever. "You have read," says Chalmers, "of certain venomous animals which expire the moment they have deposited their sting and its mortal poison in the body of their victim; and thus there ensues a double death, the death of the sufferer and the death also of the assailant. And certain it is that on the cross of our Saviour there was just such a catastrophe. There did Christ pour out his soul under the weight and agony of the exactions that were laid on him by the law; but there also did the law expend all its power as a judge and an avenger over those who believe in the Saviour."

Jesus saves from the *dominion of sin*. Perfection is not to be reached on earth. In the ripest saint there are manifold frailties. The spirit lusteth against the flesh, and the flesh against the spirit. The atmosphere of earth is tainted, and all who breathe it are impure.

But truly believe in the Lord Jesus Christ, and the power of sin will be broken within you. You will be no longer a slave, but free. Through the grace imparted to you, you will be enabled to struggle successfully with temptation, and to run the race set before you. Not that you will ever be what you will long to be while you remain in this world; but you will be in a measure holy now, and there will await you in a great and glorious eternity complete and stainless purity. "The gospel," says one, "runs in two golden streams—pardon of sin and purity of walking." They run undividedly all along in one channel, yet without confusion one with the other, as it is reported of some great rivers that run together between the same banks, and yet retain distinct colors. These streams that make glad the city of God never part one from another; if they be divided, they cease to be.

Jesus saves from all *the dread consequences of sin.*

What a dark and terrible future is before the sinner! You cannot conceive its misery. To be a castaway from God and happiness and

heaven, and to be banished to the regions of a
hopeless hell, such is the doom hanging over
the sinner. But Christ is the deliverer from
the wrath to come. Give yourself up heartily
to him, and you will have no cause to dread
the realities of the unseen world; you will be
enabled to contemplate eternity without one
shrinking fear; you will walk the dark valley
with the peace-giving persuasion that all will
be well with you.

What think you of Jesus? He is your salvation; make him your desire; count him the
chief among ten thousand; yield yourself un-
reservedly to him, and then you will know in
your own happy experience the power and
blessedness of his name.

> How sweet the name of Jesus sounds
>　　In a believer's ear!
> It soothes his sorrows, heals his wounds,
>　　And drives away his fear.
>
> It makes the wounded spirit whole,
>　　And calms the troubled breast:
> 'T is manna to the hungry soul,
>　　And to the weary rest.

IX.

THE REFUGE.

" That by two immutable things, in which it was impossible for God to lie, we might have a strong consolation, who have fled for refuge to lay hold upon the hope set before us." HEB. 6:18.

You may remember something about the old cities of refuge. Three of them were on the east, and three of them were on the west of the Jordan. A manslayer might flee into one of them, and when he entered the gate he was safe. If on examination it was found that he was the accidental cause of death, he remained secure from harm till the death of the high-priest. He was then permitted to return to his home. You have here a figure of the spiritual protection provided in the gospel for all who flee for refuge to the Lord Jesus Christ.

The cities of refuge were of *Divine appointment*. Moses and Aaron in establishing them were merely carrying out the command of God. Thus spake the Lord: so run the terms of their

appointment. And so with the gospel refuge.
Whence flows the security of those who seek
shelter in it? It has been devised by the wisdom, and reared by the power of God. "God
so loved the world, that he gave his only be-
gotten Son, that whosoever believeth in him
should not perish, but have everlasting life."

Again, the cities of refuge were *provisions
against imminent peril.* A man was in danger
of his life. Death was at his heels. He might
at any moment be slain. But once within the
sacred precincts of the city, security enclosed
him in her arms. And so with the gospel refuge. The sinner is in danger. He is pursued,
as truly as the man-slayer was. Vengeance
presses on his heels. The arm of divine justice,
is stretched out to lay him low. If the glitter-
ing sword fall, how unutterably fearful his destiny. O God, thou only knowest what is in-
volved in the loss of an undying soul. But let
him flee to the refuge, and he is quite secure.
Justice, Satan, a violated law, cannot touch
him. To all his adversaries he may boldly
say, "Who shall lay any thing to the charge of
God's elect?"

The cities of refuge were *large enough for all.* We do not know the exact size of them. They would not need to be of any great extent. But they had never to be closed against any one for want of room. And so with the gospel refuge. How many have found shelter there! An exceeding great multitude which no man can number, are already secure. But yet there is room.

The cities of refuge were *the only place where the man-slayer* could be safe. If found anywhere else by the blood-avenger, he was in danger of his life. In the appointed place of shelter alone, was he secure. And so in regard to the gospel refuge. I have seen men trying other refuges. But these are all refuges of lies. In Christ alone can the soul be secure. Away from him there is danger on every side. You cannot move a step without peril to your soul.

The cities of refuge were *only available to those who by immediate personal effort reached them.* No time was to be lost. The man-slayer was to hasten off at once. An hour's delay might prove his death. Exertion had to

be made. Every nerve had to be strained.
The whole energies had to be put forth. Nor
could this effort be made by proxy. The man-
slayer himself had to hurry away to the appointed place of security. It would not do to
devolve the duty on another. And so with
the gospel refuge. How many are dreaming
that in regard to this no earnest effort is required. Grand and perilous mistake! It has
ruined souls without number. To be saved, a
man must put forth all his energies.

Are you in the refuge? If not, how dangerous your state while you remain as you are.
Delay no longer. Away at once, or you may
be lost. "Whatsoever thy hand findeth to do,
do it with thy might."

> Laden with guilt and full of fears,
> I fly to thee, my Lord;
> And not a glimpse of hope appears,
> But in thy written word.

X.

A PRESENT SALVATION.

"Oh taste and see that the Lord is good: blessed is the man that trusteth in him." Psa. 34:8.

Salvation is a present blessing. It is not something to be possessed only in the future, but it is to be enjoyed in a measure now. Spiritual and eternal life commences on this side of the grave, and not on the other; and you may be a partaker on earth of its blessedness.

The *great reward*, it is true, is to be had in eternity. How glorious that will be! Who can tell the fund of blessings included in the word salvation? There is deliverance from guilt—the redeemed shall bask in the sunshine of Jehovah's smile. There is freedom from ignorance—the redeemed shall know even as they are known. There is complete emancipation from the bondage of sin—the redeemed shall be holy as God is holy. There is exemp-

tion from the ills of this mortal life—the redeemed shall know no fatigue, or care, or sorrow. There is security from the fear of death—
the redeemed shall live for evermore. Most
blessed consummation! The faintest glimpse
of it may well add energy to the Christian's
faith, and brightness to the Christian's hope.

But while all this is true, salvation is to be
had *in a measure now*. A sense of pardon,
peace, holiness, joy in the Holy Ghost, communion with God—what blessings greater and
more delightful than these? They require indeed to be tasted, in order to be understood.
The worldling cannot appreciate them ; but let
the believer say for what he would give them
up. He is forgiven, justified, saved. Oh the
unutterable blessedness of such a state! A
pious minister in Scotland, being asked by a
friend during his last illness whether he thought
himself dying, answered, "Really, friend, I
care not whether I am or not; if 1 die I shall
be with God, and if I live God will be with
me."

Now this present salvation is *within your
reach*. Why should you not have it now? You

may stretch forth your hand and make it yours.
Some think it presumptuous to expect this;
they suppose they must pray much and do much
before they enter on the divine life; a long
and painful process of self-crucifixion, they fancy, must be passed through ere forgiveness can
be theirs. But it is not so: you have but to
look to the cross and rest with lively faith on
Him who died on it, and acceptance with God
is secured. Not that it is easy to do this.
Pride stands in the way; self-righteousness
stands in the way; a natural alienation of
heart from God stands in the way. But if,
with the help of divine grace, you repent of
sin and believe on the Lord Jesus Christ, you
are saved this very day. It is true that this
is but to enter on the divine life. Many a day
of battling with temptation and sin will lie
before you, if you be spared, in this world.
But still, once united by true and living faith
to Christ, you will never be cast off. You
will be enabled by help from above to hold on
your way, and in maintaining the Christian
life you will enjoy the blessedness of a present
forgiveness, and you will be kept unto the sal-

vation, the full salvation to be revealed at the last time. Pardon cannot be revoked. Once justified, you are justified for ever. No power can pluck the forgiven sinner out of the Saviour's hands.

Is present salvation yours? This I know, if you are without Christ you have to blame yourself. God is willing to give you now an interest in the Redeemer's work. Jesus is offering you now pardon, peace, eternal life. The Holy Spirit, with his still small voice, is calling you now to accept the Saviour's invitation, and yield to the Saviour's claims.

> Oh may my heart, by grace renewed,
>   Be my Redeemer's throne;
> And be my stubborn will subdued,
>   His government to own.

XI.

COME.

"Him that cometh to me I will in no wise cast out."
JOHN 6:37.

You are invited to go to Christ. How are you to go? Not literally; that cannot be. Jesus has gone away; he is on the central throne of the universe. The affairs of all worlds are under his governance. And yet you may go to him—go to him as really as if you could touch his person and live in his visible presence.

He is your great High-priest: as such he once offered himself up for sins. He stood as your surety in the most momentous of all positions. He suffered, the just for the unjust. He bore your griefs, and carried your sorrows. The Lord laid on him your iniquities. If you go to him, receive him as your Saviour, and put your trust in him, he will in no wise cast you out.

He is *infinitely able to save.* Man is power-

less to save; angels are powerless to save; but
nothing is impossible to Him. You may be
deeply sunk in sin, but he can raise you up
from the horrible pit and the miry clay. You
may be stained with sins of crimson dye, but
he can purge you and make you whiter than
the snow. A multitude which no man can
number have already been washed in his precious blood, but the cleansing virtue of that
blood is as great now as ever.

And he is *infinitely kind.* You may be a sinner of the greatest enormity; you may have
had godly parents; your teachers may have
been earnestly religious; you may have waited
on a faithful and impressive ministry; but you
may have drowned convictions in worldliness
and sin. You may have spent many a long
year in infidelity and vice; you may now stand
on the shore of a dark eternity, worn out with
sin; but you need not despair. The mercy of
the Lord reacheth unto the clouds. Christ is
still willing to receive you. Beyond all knowledge is his love. It is an ocean which no line
can fathom and no shore can bound. Sinners
as great as you he has saved, and his mercy

endureth for ever. Tell me not that your iniquities are too black to be forgiven. The blood of Jesus Christ cleanseth from all sin.

An excellent and pious man, when on his death-bed, was for some time under considerable darkness respecting his spiritual state, and said to a friend, "For all that I have preached or written, there is but one scripture I can remember or dare grip to; tell me if I dare lay the weight of my salvation upon it: 'Him that cometh to me I will in no wise cast out.'" The friend replied, "You may depend upon it, though you had a thousand salvations at hazard." It was a most true and wise reply. A man may make a promise, and may change his mind and be unwilling to perform it. Not so Christ. He is the same yesterday, to-day, and for ever. A man may make a promise, and be afterwards placed in circumstances in which he is unable to fulfil it. Not so Christ. All power in heaven and in earth is his. A man may make a promise, and may be indifferent whether it be realized or not. Not so Christ. He longs with unchanging love for your eternal weal. You may then depend on his word, though you had a thousand salvations at hazard.

Do not distrust the Saviour's promise. Take him at his word. You may rely on him with assured confidence. "This man receiveth sinners." You may be deeply unworthy; you may have wandered from him ever so far; you may have brought discredit by many a year of worldliness and sin on the name of Christian; but Jesus is waiting to be gracious. He invites, encourages, beseeches you to come to him; and you may be sure that if you do so he will prove true to his promise, and never cast you out.

> Just as I am, thou wilt receive;
> Wilt welcome, pardon, cleanse, relieve:
> Because thy promise I believe,
> O Lamb of God, I come!

XII.

NOW.

"Behold, now is the accepted time; behold, now is the day of salvation." 2 Cor. 6:2.

MAKE sure of a saving interest in Christ now. Why delay? Procrastination is dangerous. In a matter which concerns you so much, it is unutterable folly to put off. Surely it is the part of a wise man to have the grand concerns of his eternity settled at once.

Delay has a *hardening tendency*. Comparatively few are converted when old. The truth does not easily penetrate the thick coating of worldliness wherewith the souls of such are encrusted. It is when the heart is soft and tender that impressions are generally made on it. We must not limit the grace of God; but every one knows that that grace commonly acts upon the young and unhardened mind.

Through delay *God may withdraw his Spirit*. That Spirit may have been long striving with

you. For years you may have felt its draw-
ings. It may have been moving and urging
you to turn unto the Lord. You may some-
times have been convinced of the vast importance of the soul and eternity; you may have
resolved and reresolved to give yourself up to
a life of decided godliness; you may have gone
on your knees and vowed to be the Lord's.
All this has been through the workings of the
Spirit within you. But you have resisted the
Spirit. Instead of cherishing his influences,
you have done your best to quench them: and
you are still unsaved. What if God should
say, "He is joined to idols; let him alone!"
How disastrous would be the issue in such a
case! The soul would be left in a state of
hopeless impenitence and unbelief.

By delay you are *losing the purest happiness.*
Perhaps you count decided religion a gloomy
thing. You fancy that it is associated with
all that is severe and repulsive; you suppose
that it calls for the giving up of every thing
that conduces to happiness; but this is a great
mistake. Never will you know what true
peace is till you cordially embrace the Saviour.

You feel a want, a deep, constant want, in your present condition; and what can fill that void but Jesus Christ? Ask those who have heartily given themselves to Christ, what they think of his service. With one voice will they reply, that they deem such service perfect freedom. Matthew Henry, a little before his death, said to a friend, "You have been used to take notice of the sayings of dying men; this is mine: that a life spent in the service of God and communion with him, is the most comfortable and happy life that any one can live in this world."

By delay you are *missing the most favorable opportunities* of being saved. In times of awakening, what loud calls are given to turn to the Lord. Solemn warnings and precious invitations without number are then addressed to you. Others around are being converted. There is a great concern about religion among all classes of society. Never was there so much anxiety about the soul and eternity. Are you unmoved and unstirred by this? If so, then the probability is, you will never be moved and stirred at all. It looks as if you were given over to judicial blindness of mind and hardness of heart.

Death may at any moment cut you down, and the delay *will prove your ruin.* Can you count on an hour more being given you? To-morrow you may be in eternity, where no message of mercy is ever heard. Some, says one, never begin to pray till God has ceased to hear. Are you keeping away from Christ? Are you still unpardoned? Are you not yet prepared to meet your God? Along the street By-and-by, one gets to the house of Never. It has been so with multitudes. How terrible the thought. It may be so with you.

Hasten, sinner, to be wise,
  Stay not for the morrow's sun;
Wisdom warns you from the skies,
  All the paths of death to shun.

Hasten mercy to implore;
  Stay not for to-morrow's sun;
Lest thy season should be o'er
  Ere to-morrow is begun.

XIII.

BUT—

"Lord, I will follow thee; but—" Luke 9:61.

Do you see the importance of deciding for Christ? Are you convinced that you ought to give yourself up to his service? Is the feeling strong within you that you should enter on an earnestly religious life? What then hinders you? Surely it must be something very serious. Christ demands an entire self-surrender; any thing else he will not accept. But you are hesitating; and why?

It may be from *the engrossment and pressure of worldly cares.* Your mind and heart are full; you are busy with earthly pursuits; you live in a scene of bustle and hurry; every hour has its work; you fancy no time can be spared for Christ: but how vain a notion. Earnest religion does not require you to neglect your business—to be uninterested in worldly pursuits—to lead a dull hermit's life. On the

contrary, it calls you to enter heartily into all
the ordinary duties of life.   But while in the
world, the Christian is not to be of the world.
And to think of a man allowing himself to be
taken up with the interests of time to the neglect of the grand concerns of eternity!   What
shall it profit a man, if he gain the whole world
and lose his own soul?

It may be *you shrink from the self-denial of
the Christian life.*   No doubt the gate is wide
enough to admit any sinner, but it is too narrow for the admission of any sin.   If you would
be decided, you must at once abandon every
known evil way, and you must seek to have
your whole life conformed to the will of God.
But should you shrink from such a life as this?
No doubt it is hard to maintain it; it is trying
often to flesh and blood; it needs a daily spirit
of self-crucifixion.   But the Redeemer's grace
is within the believer's reach.   With daily sup-
plies of it, Christ's yoke is easy and his burden
light.   And how deep and pure the inward
satisfaction a true Christian life brings along
with it!   It has joys of which the worldling
knows nothing.   Godliness is great gain even

now. "Are you happy?" was the question put one day to a beggar-boy; to which he replied at once, "I have God for my Father; I have Christ for my Redeemer; I have heaven for my inheritance. I AM happy."

It may be *you fear Christ will not accept you.* You have sinned grievously; you have broken many a vow and left unfulfilled many a resolution; you are verily guilty before God. But Christ came not to call the righteous, but sinners to repentance. "There are two things," said John Newton, "I try never to forget: first, that I am a great sinner; secondly, that Jesus is a great Saviour."

It may be you suppose you *could never lead an earnest religious life.* You are very weak; you are so ready to give way to temptation; you fall day by day into acts of sin. But has not God promised to give us help in our every time of need, if we humbly, earnestly, and perseveringly seek it? "He giveth power to the faint, and to them that have no might he increaseth strength."

It may be you do not decide *from sheer procrastination.* Oh this delay, how many souls it has ruined! They have thought; they have intended; they have determined; but they have put off. Death has come at an unexpected hour, and they are lost.

Let there be no *but*. Let there be a prompt and immediate decision. Let this be the time of your entering into a covenant with God—a covenant that shall never be forgotten. Your present convictions are of the weightiest moment. They may pass away, and leave you as unconcerned about salvation as ever you were before. Should it be so, and should you never be awakened again, how fearful to think in eternity on the time when you were *almost* converted and saved.

> Great God, on what a slender thread
> Hang everlasting things!
> Th' eternal state of all the dead
> Upon life's feeble strings.

XIV.

A FULL SURRENDER.

"My son, give me thy heart." PROV. 23:26.

MAKE a full surrender; keep back nothing; give yourself up wholly to the Lord. He will not be satisfied with any thing short of your entire being. All that you are and all that you have are his; and if you do as he requires, you will devote yourself heartily to him.

A full surrender is the *only safe course*. There can be no security without it. An unwillingness to abandon all for Christ, betrays a lingering love of self and the world. With half-heartedness God cannot be pleased. Satan would persuade you that it is enough. He has not been able to prevent your being anxious. In spite of all his endeavors to keep you asleep, you have waked to a sense of your guilt and danger; you have become alive to the vast importance of the soul and eternity. But he would urge you to a partial sacrifice. He would persuade you that you may enjoy

the world as you did before, and be religious
too. He would convince you that there is no
necessity of taking any decided step, and being different from what you were. But all
this is hollow sophistry. Be on your guard
against his devices; heed not his suggestions.
See how God would have you act. Halting
between two opinions is emphatically con-
demned. Against those who are neither cold
nor hot a terrible judgment is threatened.
And Jesus Christ says, "He that is not with
me is against me; and he that gathereth not
with me scattereth abroad."

A full surrender is the *only happy course.*
Would you have solid peace? Would you know
what true spiritual joy is? Would you possess
assurance of the divine favor and a good firm
hope of eternal life? There must be decision.
An attempted neutrality is a foe to all happiness. Never can you enjoy religion without an
entire and thorough giving up of yourself to
God. In an undecided life there is much to
dim the spiritual vision, and to disturb the
spiritual peace. A single evil desire indulged
is sufficient to rob you of happiness.

A full surrender is the *only course conducive to holiness.* Do you long to walk with God? Do you long to grow in grace? Do you long to be such as you ought to be? Then give yourself up wholly to Christ. Open your whole heart to the influx of heaven's affections. Seek to live wholly under the presiding authority of heaven's principles. Let it be your honest endeavor to breathe wholly the spirit of heaven's Lord. Then you cannot fail to advance; you will go from strength to strength; you will appear at length before God in Zion.

A full surrender is needed *to commend the religion of Christ to the world.* Alas, for the numbers of professing disciples who are neither one thing nor another. They are cautious, selfish, worldly. They do n't commit themselves. They hope they do no harm, but they certainly do no good. They are afraid to confess Christ, and they are afraid to deny him. They are idle, useless, undecided. How is the world to be impressed by such men as these? They put forth no effort for the good of their fellow-men. But make a full surrender to Christ, and yours will be no such life. You will be one with him; you will walk with him; you will gather with him. Something within you will prompt and stir to holy toils for Christ, and men will see in you the beauty of holiness. As living epistles of Christ you will be seen and read of all men.

Do you hesitate to make a full surrender? Think well indeed on what you are about to do. Count the cost. Consider the nature and character and conditions of the service of Christ. Do this, and then deliberately and solemnly decide. Let this be your resolve on your knees at the throne of grace:

I take God as my Father;

I take Christ as my only Saviour;

I take the Holy Ghost as my Sanctifier and Guide.

All my being I give up to the Three-One God.

> Just as I am—thy love unknown
> Has broken every barrier down;
> Now to be thine, yea, thine alone,
> O Lamb of God, I come.

XV.

BORN AGAIN.

" Jesus answered and said unto him, Verily, verily, I say unto thee, Except a man be born again, he cannot see the kingdom of God." JOHN 3:3.

ARE you born again? My question is a most solemn one. Think earnestly on it; it concerns your eternal interests. He that is born once only, as has been said, dies twice; but he that is born twice, dies only once, for over him the second death hath no power.

In those who are born again there takes place a *great, inward, divinely wrought change.* It is a *great* change. The new-born soul passes from death to life. It has views, feelings, desires, hopes, fears, joys, sorrows, which it had not before; its whole nature is renewed. Again, it is an *inward* change. The heart loves what it did not love before, hates what it did not hate before, desires what it did not desire before. Once more, it is a *divinely wrought* change. No human power can work it; sermons cannot work it; Bible reading and prayers cannot work it; sacraments cannot work it. You may try hard to work it in yourself or in others; but the Spirit of the living God, he and he alone can produce this saving change.

A man *must be born again, or be lost.* The statement is no rash one; I can make it good. The authority of Scripture is my warrant for it. You believe that Jesus is the Son of God; you believe that he cannot lie; you believe that heaven and earth may pass away, but that his word will never pass away. Well, what saith he? "Verily, verily, I say unto thee, Except a man be born again, he cannot see the kingdom of God." Be sure, then, that the gate of heaven will be for ever barred against the unregenerate.

Certain marks distinguish those who are born again. They *hate sin;* they feel it to be a burden; they long to be wholly free from it. They *habitually seek after holiness;* they desire to be clothed with it; they will never be satisfied without it. They are *spiritually minded.* The

ordinary cares and business of life necessarily
occupy much of their attention, but their treas-
ure is in heaven and their heart is also there.
They *seek to act up to their profession.* The duties of the sphere in which Providence has
placed them they endeavor faithfully to perform. They desire to be diligent in business,
fervent in spirit, serving the Lord. They *are
making progress in the divine life.* This progress may not always be clear and steady, but
it is true and real. Such are a few of the
marks which distinguish those who are born
again. They do not appear with equal clear-
ness in all the children of God. But if a
man cannot discover any signs of them in his
heart and life, he has good grounds for fearing
that the great change has not yet taken place
in him.

How is it with your soul? Many are dreaming that if they be guilty of no gross and open
sins; if they be respectable members of society; if they make a fair profession, all is sure
to be well with them in the future. But this is
a grand delusion; for *the Book,* in the plainest
terms, declares that a man must be born again,

or be lost.   Are you born again?   If so, there
is but a breath between you and heaven; if not
so, there is but a breath between you and hell.
And let no one say, We must wait God's time.
God's time is now.   Apply at once for his re-
generating grace, and it will not be refused.

The words which an old minister had graven
on his tombstone are faithful and true: "Remember, no salvation without a new birth.
Surely they that are not born again shall one
day wish they had never been born at all."

> Let songs of praises fill the sky:
>   Christ, our ascended Lord,
> Sends down his Spirit from on high,
>   According to his word.

XVI.

A CHRISTIAN.

"That worthy name by the which ye are called."
JAMES 2:7.

IF you are born again, and have made a full surrender of yourself to Jesus, you are a Christian. Holy and honorable name. No title is more to be prized. Men covet earthly distinctions. What labors and sacrifices they undergo to secure them! But here is a name nobler far. Who are entitled to bear it?

A Christian is one who *believes in the Divinity of Christ.* Jesus was indeed a man. He had a nature like ours. He was often hungry and thirsty and weary. He was born; he suffered; he died. But though finite, he was also infinite; though very man, he was also very God. Divine names are given him; divine attributes are ascribed to him; divine works were performed by him; divine worship is paid to him; divine honors clothe him. He was Emmanuel, God with us.

A Christian is one who *rests on the atonement of Christ* for acceptance with God. Some look upon Christ as a teacher; and no doubt he was a teacher—the greatest teacher the world ever saw. Others look upon Christ as a martyr; and no doubt he was a martyr, for he sealed his testimony with his blood. Others look upon Christ as an example; and no doubt he was a pattern—the great model man. But above all this, Christ was a great atoning sacrifice. You know from experience the blessedness of this truth; for if a real Christian, you are prepared to make it as your confession:

> I the chief of sinners am,
> But Jesus died for me.

A Christian is one *who loves Christ and longs to be like him.* There are some who need only to be known to be loved. How preëminently is this the case with Jesus Christ. To them who believe in him he is precious; and loving his Lord, the Christian longs to resemble him. What was his character when he was upon earth? He was pure, spotless, perfect; and what believer does not desire to be so too?

A Christian *confesses Christ.* Many act as

if they were ashamed of him; they shrink from
showing themselves his decided followers;
they cannot bear the idea of being different
from others; they would rather endure any
thing than be counted singular, or be called
hypocrites by an unthinking world; they have
not the courage to stand up for Christ. By
many an act of inconsistency and lukewarm-
ness they bring discredit on the name they
bear. Let it not be so with you. Beware of
allowing any one for a moment to imagine that
you are ashamed of Christ:

> Ashamed of Jesus, that dear Friend
> On whom my hopes of heaven depend!
> No; when I blush be this my shame,
> That I no more revere his name.

A Christian *waits and longs for Christ's unveiled
presence in glory.* This earth is the worldling's
all. His heart is set on its business and pleasures and friendships. Give him these, and he
asks nothing more. But how different with a
living Christian! He regards this world as
but a lodging-house—a tent that is to be taken
down. Beyond the stars is his spirit's true
home; and he never expects to be fully happy

till he gets there. And what, to him, is the grand anticipated charm of heaven? the unveiled presence of the Lord Jesus Christ.

Walk worthy of your high calling. Live near to Christ. Let it be your most earnest desire to get closer and closer to him; to enter more and more into his heart; and to be filled more and more with his spirit. Be ever longing after higher attainments in holiness. Seek to have your path like the shining light, that shineth more and more unto the perfect day.

Let Christ, to whom we now belong,
 His sovereign right assert;
To him we owe the grateful song,
 To him the loving heart.

He justly claims us for his own,
 Who bought us with a price;
The Christian lives to Christ alone,
 To Christ alone he dies.

XVII.

SECRET THINGS.

"The secret things belong unto the Lord our God; but those things which are revealed belong unto us and to our children for ever, that we may do all the words of this law." DEUT. 29:29.

You are surrounded with mysteries in the world. You meet with them above you, around you, within you. In every blade of grass, in every insect that flutters in the sunbeam, in every beating heart, there is much you cannot understand. Knowledge has indeed made mighty progress; and yet there are multitudes of secret things on all sides of us which nature has not whispered in the ear of her most ardent votaries. And so in providence there are many mysteries. We cannot see at present the whys and wherefores of God's dealings with men. Clouds and darkness are round about him. In the Bible too there are mysteries which the mind of man cannot grasp. Be not disquieted and perplexed with these; a day of revelation will come.

It was *to be expected* that there would be hidden things in the Bible. It is the book of God. And who is he? A Being altogether different from us—infinite, unsearchable, eternal. Was it not to be looked for, then, that in a communication from him there would be some things dark and hard to be understood? A child is not able to comprehend all that is said to it by its parent; surely then it is not strange that we in our present condition—the very infancy of our being—should not be able fully to comprehend the revelation of the Infinite. Accordingly there are domains of truth which are accessible only to God. We are permitted to enter the antechamber; but we are not allowed to penetrate the recesses of the sanctury. Till we pass within the veil, and have our powers of vision strengthened, we must be content to wait.

The mysteries of revelation *are useful.* They teach us a lesson *of faith.* The child takes much in trust from his father; and so God would have us repose thorough confidence in him, and believe what we cannot now understand or explain. They teach us also a lesson *of patience.* All will be cleared up at length. Light will be shed on the dark things of God. In eternity more may be learned in an hour than can be learned in a whole lifetime now. We should quietly wait till then. They teach us, moreover, a lesson *of hope.* A bright and blessed day is coming. Soon will the morning break and the shadows flee away, and then what discoveries will be made! Let the heart be stirred by the prospect. We shall know even as we are known.

While there are mysteries in the Bible, *all that is necessary for us to know* has been plainly revealed. It tells us plainly of the evil of sin. It tells us plainly of a divinely appointed and divinely accomplished Saviour. It tells us plainly of the necessity of repentance, faith, and holiness. It tells us plainly of the vast importance of giving immediate heed to the things which belong to our peace. It tells us plainly of an everlasting heaven and an everlasting hell, and how we may secure the one and escape the other.

These and such like truths are clearly revealed. There is no mystery about them. They are written as with a sunbeam on the page of Scripture; and it is the dictate of true wisdom not to suffer what we know to be disturbed by what we know not.

Attend to the things which belong to you. Act from day to day simple faith in Christ. Set yourself earnestly to the performance of all plainly commanded duty. Be not harassed by the dark truths of revelation, but seek to conquer all known truth. Remember that you are but in the first stage of your existence, and look forward hopefully to a time when, endowed with loftier powers than those you now possess, you will be privileged to make discoveries which it has not entered into the heart of man to conceive.

> Such are the hopes that cheer the saint;
> These hopes their God hath given.
> His Spirit is the earnest now,
> And seals their souls for heaven.

XVIII.

THE RACE.

"So run, that ye may obtain." 1 Cor. 9:24.

You have a race to run. You have to put forth all your energies. Only thus can you reach the goal, and win the immortal prize. Think not that when once converted you may be at your ease. You only begin the Christian race at the cross; and it is not done till you reach your dying day.

Consider the *points of resemblance between your life and a race.* In a race a certain *course is marked out.* Over it the competitors have to run. On no account must they deviate from it. And so in the Christian life. There is a course marked out for you. It is the narrow way of holiness. Again, in the race *there is required laborious exertion.* It is no easy matter to reach the goal before all others. In order to this every nerve has to be strained. And so in the Christian life. You must bear in

mind that of yourself you can do nothing; that
it is not of him that willeth, nor of him that
runneth, but of God that showeth mercy. And
yet you must act with all the ardor of such as
believe that success depends on their own exer-
tions. In the race *a prize is held out* to the successful competitor. It may be of no great value
in itself, but it is looked upon as a sign of dis-
tinction, and is coveted by many. Willing-
ly do they put themselves to toil and trouble to secure it, and great is their delight if
they succeed. And so in the Christian life.
A prize is held out to the successful candidate—
a crown of glory that fadeth not away. Here
is a reward worth the struggling for. No time
can impair its value; but on the contrary, it
shall grow in ever-brightening splendor from
age to age.   .

And *how are you to run this race?* They who
run a race make themselves *as light as possible.*
They put off whatever might encumber them,
and they train themselves anxiously before-
hand for the contest; and so should it be in
the Christian race. You should lay aside
every weight, and the sin that doth most easily

beset you; and you should count no sacrifice too dear so that you may win heaven. Again, they who run a race are required to *exercise patience*. It may be necessary to submit to self-denying discipline, and on the day of trial they must steadily and perseveringly hold on till the goal is reached. And so in the Christian race. If you would gain the promised prize you must be patient. You must not faint or be discouraged by the obstacles which you meet with in your progress; but in the face of every difficulty you must press onwards to the goal. And once more, they who run a race are often stimulated to increased and strenuous effort by *the presence of others* who have former-ly won the prize. And you are to look to Jesus. You are to look to him as your great Example, who has run the race before you; and you are to look to him as your almighty Friend, who is ever able and ready to help you, so that you may run and not be weary.

And *why* should you thus run the Christian race? *God calls on you to do it;* and he that knows his Lord's will, and does not do it, shall be beaten with many stripes. Moreover the *prize is certain* if you heartily engage in this race. In respect to the pursuit of earthly good, you may reckon on meeting with sore disappointments; but the immortal crown is sure to every truly earnest runner. Besides, *the prize*, as I would remind you again, *is of priceless value.* It is no corruptible and unsubstantial thing. Human tongue cannot express its worth. It is salvation; it is eternal life; it is an enduring inheritance; it is an exceeding, even an eternal weight of glory; it is heaven.

So run that you may obtain. Press on towards the mark for the prize of your high calling. Be not discouraged because of the way. Animated by the thought of the many who have arrived at the goal, go on with growing ardor, and you will at length be partaker of their surpassing glory and their satisfying joy.

> Awake, my soul, stretch every nerve,
> And press with vigor on;
> A heavenly race demands thy zeal,
> And an immortal crown.

XIX.

REDEEMING THE TIME.

" Redeeming the time, because the days are evil."
Ephes. 5:16.

Time is the most precious of all your posses-
sions. With it nothing which you have may
be compared in value. It stands prominently
out as of unspeakable importance. And how
is it so precious? The use you make of it is
to determine the character of your eternity.
And yet how much is it misspent by the great
bulk of men! No note is taken of it as it hur-
ries along. Its vast importance is forgotten.
Days and months of it are allowed to pass un-
heeded. It is short, very short; but to many
it appears long and tedious. It hangs heavily
on their hands; they know not how to use it:
ingenuity is exercised in finding out ways and
means to kill it. Very different was the esti-
mate formed of time by Paul. He saw it in its
proper light; and viewing it as the spring-time
of eternity, he often reminds his converts of its

transitoriness, and calls on them to use all dili-
gence and earnestness in redeeming it—hus-
banding it, improving it, employing it in such
a manner as to attain in it the purposes for
which it has been given.

Remember that time is *a great reality.* We
are apt to regard it as something unsubstantial
and shadowy. It seems to possess no true existence. In what light do we commonly view
it but as thin air, or rather as empty space?
But seek to have a clear, distinct, abiding sense
of its reality. And in order to this, cultivate
the habit of thinking from day to day what you
can do in the way of improving it.

Remember that time is *inseparably connected
with eternity.* Do not forget this most solemn
relation. Each little portion of your present
existence has to do with the interminable future
that awaits you. It is so indeed. There will
be nothing in eternity to you but what springs
out of time. Is there good in the world
unseen? Are there joys of which the mind
while here has no conception? Are there
sentient and spiritual delights suited to a fully
regenerated body and to a fully regenerated

soul? All this will be realized in consequence of the right use of time. Is there evil in the world unseen? Are there miseries there unspeakably woful? Is there a worm that dieth not, and a fire that shall never be quenched? All this will be realized in consequence of the abuse of time. "Be not deceived; God is not mocked: for whatsoever a man soweth, that shall he also reap. For he that soweth to his flesh shall of the flesh reap corruption; but he that soweth to the Spirit shall of the Spirit reap life everlasting."

Remember too that time is *short, uncertain,* and *irrevocable.* It is *short.* How small and short-lived the objects to which it is likened in holy writ! It is spoken of as a span, as a vapor, as a cloud, as a step, as the fading flower. It is *uncertain.* The present is yours, but in the future you have no ascertained property. You know not what a day will bring forth; there may be but a step between you and death. This very night your soul may be required of you. Work heartily for God and the soul and eternity now; to-morrow you may have no opportunity to do so. Once more, time is *ir-*

revocable. The clock is wound up once for all; yet a little while and its last hour will strike for you. Many things when lost may be recovered, but not so with time. Over the past you have no control. It is departed. No power can bring it back.

Redeem the time. Lost years, a coming judgment-seat, the glory of God, call you with loud voice to do so. If your soul be at peace through faith in Jesus Christ, and if the Holy Ghost have begun a good work in you, work out your salvation with fear and trembling, and live heartily for God. The night is far spent, and the day is at hand; soon will the clouds part their awful folds. The realities of eternity will ere long break upon your view, and then all opportunities of working for God in a sinful world will be for ever gone.

> Dear Lord, and shall we ever live
>   At this poor dying rate—
> Our love so faint, so cold to thee,
>   And thine to us so great!
>
> Come, Holy Spirit, heavenly Dove,
>   With all thy quickening powers;
> Come, shed abroad a Saviour's love,
>   And that shall kindle ours.

XX.

AN UNCHANGEABLE SAVIOUR.

"Jesus Christ the same yesterday, and to-day, and
for ever." HEB. 13:8.

ALL things seem to be subject to change.
Above us the stars have shone for ages; but
they shall fall as a fig-tree casteth her untimely
figs. Around us the hills have stood for cen-
turies; but the mountains shall depart, and the
hills be removed. Beneath us lies the firm and
solid earth; but in the fulness of time it shall
be burned up. In respect to man, one generation passeth away and another generation cometh. The little history of every one is an ever-
varying, ever-shifting scene; but how delightful the thought that there is One at least with
whom it is not thus. Here is a refuge for the
soul amid the transitory objects of time and
sense. The changes in heaven, on earth, in
man, produce no change in Christ; for he is
the same yesterday, and to-day, and for ever.

Jesus is *unchangeable in his being.* When on

earth, he was very man. He had all the sinless infirmities of our nature; he was bone of
our bone and flesh of our flesh: but he was
also very God; and in his Godhead he must
be unchangeable. Were he to change, it would
be for the better or for the worse. But he
cannot change for the better, for this would
imply previous imperfection; nor can he change
for the worse, for then would he cease to be
the all-perfect One. As God then he must be
ever the same—the same in his being and glory
and blessedness, possessed of every possible
perfection in the highest possible degree.

Christ is *unchangeable in his attributes.* How
great *his power* on earth! See him amid the
wrecks of humanity: the blind received their
sight, the lame walked, the lepers were cleans-
ed. See him in the domains of death: the
corpse started to life at his word. See him
amid the fury of the tempest: he rebuked the
wind, and there was a great calm. And he is
still the same: he can cure all our spiritual
ills; he can quicken such as are dead in tres-
passes and sins; he can bid all our fears and
troubles cease. How great *his wisdom* on

earth—a wisdom which he exercised so gra-
ciously on behalf of his disciples.   And he is
still the same: with implicit confidence may
his people trust in him as an unerring guide.
How great *his love !* Ever did he pardon the
penitent, strengthen the feeble, comfort the
bowed-down.   And he is still the same: no
change has come over his kind, tender, loving
heart; never will he send the humble and
weary empty away.

Christ is *unchangeable in his doctrines.* The
ideas, feelings, purposes of men often vary;
but an infinite Being knows no mutability.
New thoughts cannot start up in the mind of
God.   Now what are the grand leading doctrines of the gospel of Christ ? We must repent of sin ; we must rest on Jesus by a true
and living faith; we must be renewed by the
Spirit of God.   It must be thus with us if we
would be saved.   There can be no doubt whatever that this is most plainly announced.   Any
other way of getting to heaven is obviously
out of the question.   There are myriads now
in glory.   Ten thousand times ten thousand,
and thousands of thousands have reached the

paradise of God. They form an exceeding great multitude, which no man can number. By no other way can we join that glorious company than through repentance, faith, renewal.

Think of it, Christ is unchangeable in his *being*. How delightful the thought! If resting on him, you are on solid ground. Feeble and mortal though you be, you are a partaker of Christ's own stability. Your feet are on a rock, and you cannot be moved. Christ is unchangeable in his *attributes*. Fear not. Trust in him. Cast the whole burden of your being upon him. He is able and willing to help you in your every time of need, if you depend on him. Christ is unchangeable in his *doctrines*. Have you truly repented of sin? Have you been led to the cross and given up yourself to Jesus? Have you been born again through the Holy Ghost? Most solemn questions! Blessed are all they who can answer them aright.

And Oh, when I have safely passed
Through every conflict but the last,
Still, Lord, unchanging, watch beside
My bed of death—for thou hast died.

XXI.

THE DAY OF SMALL THINGS.

"Who hath despised the day of small things!"
Zech. 4:10.

Have you been brought out of darkness?
Does the true light now shine in and around
you? Are you a child of the day? But is
your faith feeble? Is your love cold? Is
your zeal fitful and languid? Be not cast
down; take heart. Do not despise the day of
small things.

It is well to long for progress in spiritual attainment. A great work of holiness has to be
wrought in you; and now is the time to have
it done. What is the future that awaits you?
You are to mingle with those whose robes are
white. You are to sit with angels. You are
to stand in the presence of God and the Lamb.
Do you feel unprepared for such a state? Aim
at progress; long and pray for progress; be
not content without progress. Seek to have

your path like the shining light, that shineth more and more unto the perfect day.

But *be not discouraged.* Has the word of life been received into a true and honest heart? It will work, and work, and work. Nor will it cease its effectual working till the whole man is brought into obedience to it. But this is not to be the result of a day or month or year. A lifetime is needed for the attainment of holiness in any very high degree. Hear what the great Augustine says: " Is love made perfect the moment it is born? So far from this, it is born in order to be brought to perfection. When it has been born it is nourished; when it has been nourished it is strengthened; when it has been strengthened it is made perfect; when it has arrived at perfection it says, I desire to depart and to be with Christ." It is well to mourn over the dimness of your views and the faintness of your love, and the worldliness of your thoughts; but the Lord Jesus is very pitiful. He knows your frame, and remembers that you are dust; and he will not break the bruised reed, nor quench the smoking flax. Think not that if you be truly his, he will cast you off. Though he had found you as black as hell, he will present you at length before God without spot, or wrinkle, or any such thing.

To stimulate you, I would bid you *look to those who have gone before you.* "I often contemplate," says Foster, "and with the due amazement, Moses, Elijah, Paul, and John, with the rest who have formed the first and noblest rank of mankind. I have wondered whether there is in the nature of things an impossibility of ever approaching them; but I have concluded with warmth that all things should be attempted, should be suffered, should be sacrificed in the divine emulation of emulating them." And if they were great on earth, how glorious are they now! They have been delivered from the bondage of corruption. They have triumphed over all the ills incident to humanity. They have reached a state of absolute security, happiness, perfection. But you may attain a position as glorious as theirs. By the same grand process of faith and inward renewal you may be perfect as they are perfect.

It is the day of small things, but rejoice in

the assurance that a day of great things is coming. There is first the blade, then the ear, then the full corn in the ear. There are first the totterings of infancy, then the steady walk of manhood. There is first the dawn, then the twilight, then the perfect day.

> Oh long expected day, begin;
> Dawn on these realms of woe and sin:
> Fain would I leave this weary road,
> And sleep in death to rest with God.

XXII.

THE FINAL DAY.

"For we must all appear before the judgment-seat of Christ." 2 COR. 5:10.

A DAY of judgment is coming. It may still be far distant, or it may be nearer at hand; but arrive it certainly shall. There is to be a winding up of the affairs of earth. The curtain is to fall on the things of time, and there shall be unfolded to mortal eye the visions of eternity.

How will that day *begin?* The loud peal of the Archangel's trump will announce its arrival. Previous to this no strange phenomena may have served to indicate its near approach; but how solemn the scenes which shall then be witnessed! The sun shall grow dim in heaven; the stars shall pale their feeble light; the elements shall melt with fervent heat; the foundations of the earth shall tremble: nature shall heave her final groan. The living, what of them? We are told they shall suddenly be

changed. The dead, what of them? They
who sleep shall suddenly awake. All who
tread, or who have ever trod the earth shall
hurry, moved by some resistless impulse, to the
great white throne of the descending Judge.
"Every eye shall see him." "Before him shall
be gathered all nations." "I saw the dead,
small and great, stand before God."

How is that day to be *spent?*

It is to be the great reckoning-time. We
are to give in our account. Each one for himself is to answer for his life on earth, and is to
receive the things done in his body, according
to that he hath done, whether it be good or
bad. How are the myriads who have peopled
the world to be tried? How are the thoughts
and words and actions of men to be unveiled
and judged? I do not know all this. It is
wrapped in mystery. I am unable to understand or explain it; but I know that God is
infinite in all his attributes, and that what is
impossible with man is possible with him. It
will be a *solemn* judgment. There will be
every thing to render it an imposing scene.
God, angels, Satan no doubt, all present; the

vast congregation at the bar ; the irrevocable
sentence passed upon myriads of myriads of
immortal beings. What can be more solemn
than all this? It will be a *searching* judgment.
The eye of Omniscience will pierce through
every spirit. It will read with unerring glance
the character engraven on all hearts. There
is nothing hidden which shall not then be
brought to light. And it will be an *individual*
judgment. Many may be the assembled thousands ; but there will be no possibility of losing ourselves in the multitude around us. We
must every one of us give in our account unto
God.

How will the day *close?*

Its end will be far from being the same to
all who are judged. To some it will end in
unutterable sorrow ; while to others it will end
in unutterable joy. The wicked "shall go away
into everlasting punishment, but the righteous
into life eternal." About that doleful region
which is to be the future abode of the former
we know but little. It is a place of ceaseless
torment—a region of hopeless misery—a land
of everlasting exile from the presence and favor

of God—an eternity of woe. Dreadful doom! And yet such is the portion of the lost. How different the lot of the saved! Salvation is theirs. And what a fund of blessings is included in that word! There is deliverance from ignorance, guilt, sin, sorrow, death; and there is the possession of every good which can gratify the human heart.

Be not forgetful of your great destiny. Make ready for the day of the Lord. Whatever else you neglect, neglect not this. Look upon it as the great business of life to glorify God, and to prepare for the solemn future which lies before you. Live so that when you receive the summons of death you may cheerfully obey it, and haste with willing step to Him in whose presence is fulness of joy, and at whose right hand there are pleasures for evermore.

> Impartial retribution then
> Our different lives await;
> Our present actions, good or bad,
> Shall fix our future state.